To Jessica –
Happy Birthday!
Much love,
Melissa

Breaking *the* Drought

Also by Stephen Levine

A Gradual Awakening

Who Dies?

Meetings at the Edge

Healing into Life and Death

Guided Meditations

Embracing the Beloved

A Year to Live

Turning Toward the Mystery

Unattended Sorrow

Breaking *the* Drought

VISIONS OF GRACE

Stephen Levine

LARSON PUBLICATIONS

BURDETT, NY

ISBN 13: 978-0-943914-48-0
ISBN 10: 0-943914-48-5

Publisher's Cataloging-In-Publication Data
(Prepared by The Donohue Group, Inc.)

Levine, Stephen, 1937-
  Breaking the drought : visions of grace / Stephen Levine.

  p. ; cm.

  ISBN-13: 978-0-943914-48-0
  ISBN-10: 0-943914-48-5

1. Spiritual life—Poetry. 2. New Age poetry. I. Title.

PS3612.E956 B74 2007
811/.54

Published by Larson Publications
4936 NYS Route 414
Burdett, NY 14818 USA
www.larsonpublications.com

17 16 15 14 13 12 11 10 09 08 07
10 9 8 7 6 5 4 3 2 1

To Ondrea my one and only for so many
incarnations in our 29 years together.

Introduction

MY FIRST BOOK OF POETRY was published in 1959. *The Village Voice* liked it and said they hoped I would write more. My next two books were small press prose poems mostly sold by City Lights Books. I related to myself with the grandiose self-proclamation of "poet" until I noticed there was a weeping in the corner of the room. It called the poetic intuition into whole different areas of service. Then, thirty-five years ago, my Buddhist meditation teachers suggested that I should teach. After a few years teaching meditation in various prisons, I began working with the dying and grieving.

Incorporating aspects of that inner work into practices for finishing business (forgiveness), deepening awareness (mindfulness), and opening the heart (compassion and loving kindness practices), I was learning to hear more deeply, to listen at the intuitive level which displayed so fruitfully many of those places I remained hidden from life and from myself. And much that went into "formal" poetry rose to the surface as insight into patients' process.

Stephen Mitchell once asked why there was, except for a few cases, such a hiatus in the publishing of my poetry. And then he, gracious as ever, nodded knowingly when I described how so much of that poetic sensibility had gone into the intuitions so helpful in tuning into patients in a time of difficulty. He acknowledged how much of the poetic he had sensed in the numerous guided meditations for various sorts of healing and insight practices that had appeared over the years.

Now decades later, breaking innumerable droughts, reawakening the subconscious to blossom from quite a different intuitive seed, nourished by retiring from working with patients and a visit from Robert Bly, another book of undecoded transmissions from the underdream has come to light.

STEPHEN LEVINE

JULY 2007

Breaking the Drought,
a reawakening

Bogged down in life,

in sickness and in health

in death do us part,

we become easy to recognize

and unreal, so much of our selves

forgetting what we set out to do.

The Southwest is eight years into a drought

Droughts can make you superstitious,
change the way you pray
and to whom.

Droughts can make you dream
of drums and magic,
make you change your religion
like Old Noah almost did
parched and trembling one night
secretly beside the burning rock
wagering his uncertain soul with God
"for just a sip from Your deep cup."

And what a flood it was!

Noah had such a big soul
and God loves a gambler
who will bet everything
to find his original heart
and break the drought.

Autumn bends the drought

There is a golden whale swimming
from mountain to mountain
across the Sangre de Cristos.
It's a two day walk along her body.
She raised her head to peek over the ridge,
fell in love with the tree line and dove
down the ravines and through the yellow aspen
to rub her belly on the valley treetops,
tail flipping over the rocky crest.

There's bear up there and elk
and hunters lost and skeletons
in winter dens and lions hiding
from thunder under the yellow leaf-fall.

All day long she rolls and breaches on the mountainside
spraying siskins and maroon-capped sparrows
from tufts of quiet pinion. Breathes in the forests
for a geologic instant, a Cambrian eon,
and sinks into the starry channels
of the ocean of neurons
behind the brow.

She promises rain . . . again.

The first substantial rains in several years

Bogged down in life,
in sickness and in health
in death do us part,
we become easy to recognize
and unreal, so much of our selves
forgetting what we set out to do.

On his decades cushion,
chin parallel to the floor,
the spine straight as inquiry will allow,
hollow as breath, he filled with fire
and peace, he filled with promise.

The possibility of rain
gathers in soft gray layers.

So many false prophets
so many near-monsoons
casting shadows as if . . . then fading away.

But perhaps not this one!

Thunder cracks open the clouds—
heads raise, the scurry stops,
lightning bleaches the dry mountain air
strobes the drooped pinion as they appear and disappear.
Beneath the hard-pan crust the thirsty
subsoil trembles like a lover in expectation.

Leaning over the edge of the gun-metal clouds the sky relents,
wets the pale pink tongue of dusty toads.
The first drops
    bouncing
        off the hard earth.

A gray fox denning in the riverbank
smells the lightning and hears the slow trickling.
From rivulets gathering upstream
a stout wave soon evicts all inhabitants.

A silver curtain of rain chasing children laughing
across the pasture. Its welcome shadow sliding over
the dead fields toward the snow capped Sangre de Cristos.
The sunset drops beneath the charcoal clouds,
blood of Christ melting the crimson snow on the mountainside
trickling through the broken rockslide
to the pale fields below, the last of the
dust devils sucking up another century of topsoil.

God comes as rain to ranchers in their living rooms
and farmers sitting with their head in their hands
on cracked pine porches, stepping off
to let the rain rinse the defeat from their faces,
walking out onto the adobe-earth that shelters
and protects them, that births and buries them.
Rain combines with earth to create and harvest us all.

A stunted stalk of last year's wheat senses itself being lifted
by the seepage beneath, monsoon rain lifting us all,
rain drumming matrilineal chants on the tin roof.

Leaving the old red truck stuck
we walk between the ruts
we leave our shoes,
bare feet are best,
mud between our toes,
to know where we stand.

The sun having crossed the orange mesa steppes
drops into the flat-topped volcano behind Georgia O'Keefe's house
and disappears into her backyard a hundred miles away.

Behind what I can not see, further on
beyond the city's yellow lights
and diamond boulevards, the farmer
a few miles on plows by last light,
by first rain, his ground at last.

The sun follows the geese west.

Thunder raises heads great and small,
the elk and the field mouse change their plans.

The great mahogany and ebony elk weaving
through the pinions and ponderosa stops,
lets the rain caress the back of his iron neck,
lifts his great head, just enough
to let the rain trickle down the furrows on his antlers.
He delights in the cool running the rim of his warm nostrils.
He raises his head higher and bellows a blessing to sentience.

First rains chasing turquoise bellied geckoes
up the stony arroyo walls.

The monsoon's return

From weathered porches expectation
explores the charcoal folds in the cotton sky.
Thunderheads ease themselves down
the slopes of the Sangre de Cristo Mountains.

We stand arms outstretched like wildcatters
who have "struck it rich" soaked
to the skin with the blood of Christ
which this day is rain.

Moses struck the rock and broke the bargain
with the deluge, he had to pay Old Noah's
bar tab for us all. Already well into history,
in Exodus, he needed only to speak kindly
for a cool drink from a warm boulder
in a vast wasteland.
But a few chapters later a disillusioned deity
needs more assurances and it took some foul language
and a pair of num-chuks to hit the headwaters
of the Nile . . . but bitter waters
confine us to our sorrows,
and it takes the sweet water of mercy
to slake the inborn thirst
and win back God's confidence,
to crack the rock
and break the drought.

It began to rain the day our dog died
and it has rained for two months since,
She would have wanted it this way
she was frightened by thunder.

Now the rains cross the meadow
and my breath changes shape
The Thunder Bird pulls free
from the underdream
and crosses dry centuries of unknowing
to land on this page.

It pecks at the rock in the mind of the last paragraph
and begins to imitate the Cretaceous song
in a manner that awakens crystals.
At first just a few words, a mantra or prayer,
sufficed but on their way to Jericho it took more
than friends in high places and
raising his staff to the origins of stone
for war not to begin another drought.

A Reawakening

The source of the Nile

How can we break the drought before we find
the source of the Nile?

    Where do we go to find the source of the Nile?

    Do we begin at the beginning or the end?

    At the hidden spring that trickled
down a stained rock face and first soaked
the dryness away? Or opening like a silk fan
at its conclusion through the undulating columns
of the Alexandrian Library, emptying the history
of history into the deep blue sea?

    If we wish to end the drought and save the ocean
for whales and lonely fishermen forlorn as fog
we must take a star map along to remember
what we are fishing for.

    I first used the Upanishads to call the wild carp,
and the Gita to bring them aboard. Gone overboard myself
and nearly drowned so many times in the mind stream.

    When our longing takes the bait the Nile rolls back up
onto itself like a yo-yo. There is an implosion, a wave running
down the optic nerve, a faint symphony approaching
resonating in the inner ear.

When Shaman Buddha fished in Shaman Jesus'
sandaled sea, and caught the fish of John,
the waters of the Nile rose further up the spine.
When Jesus walked in Elijah's footsteps across
the Red Sea it split open from habit and
the followers of a single sun emerged on
the other side.

If the Nile does not begin in the heart then where?

If the heart does not begin in the midst of mind, then where?

Because the Nile begins by remembering
something forgotten is it said its source is hidden?

If the beginning did not depend on anything,
just started of its own accord, like the first karma
whose source is said to be imponderable,
did it originate perhaps in the origin of the Big Bang,
when the first beginning floated like the crocodile god
down the Nile?

If its beginning did not depend on anything but grace
it would explain our ultimate homesickness and the river's
run through forgetfulness and compassion to whet
our appetite for more. To break the drought and ride
the raft-at-hand down the length of the Nile.

I go to the Spanish poems

I go to the Spanish poems
the way I once went to the Gita
each morning . . . they wait for me
like Arjuna waits for Krishna between the battle lines
in the space where poetry is more than art.

In that last poem I missed the sound
of the old truck straining up the mountainside,
old tires furtively grasping the hard dirt road,
the old engine sounding more like metal
with every load. The trees have left the mountain
disconsolate to become the *New York Times*.

I am drawn back and back
I am drawn into memory,
into the core of the earth where poetry remains
molten and unwritten quietly from word
to word, phrase by phrase, upward from heart to mind
like the light reaching through to the old farmer
who can see the earth breathe,
clearing another field and leaving behind a wall,
a New England poem of gray green rock and pastel stone
that will live so much longer than he,
and planting food for a lifetime or two as well.

In the company of kind men with good eyes
in the company of kind women with good hands
the road seems less difficult,
and the truck that passes headed
in the other direction has left its corpses
on a freight-wagon to the mill,
gone from the windswept mountain
to make the same headlines since great grandfather
having left Cervantes in the Old Country
dragged the first ponderosa down the mountainside
to hold up his roof.

The driver of the old truck does not feel his hands
on the old wooden wheel, verbs run along
his lifeline, nouns nestled in his palms
and beneath his tongue Andalusian love songs
and the smell of roasted vegetables
and his mother's starch.

Millennium blessing

There is a grace approaching
that we shun as much as death,
it is the completion of our birth.

It does not come in time,
    but in timelessness
when the mind sinks into the heart
and we remember.

It is an insistent grace that draws us
to the edge and beckons us surrender
safe territory and enter our enormity.

We know we must pass
    beyond knowing
and fear the shedding.

But we are pulled upward
    none-the-less
through forgotten ghosts
    and unexpected angels,
luminous.

And there is nothing left to say
but we are That.

And that is what we sing about.

Half life

We walk through half our life
as if it were a fever dream

barely touching the ground

our eyes half open
our heart half closed.

Not half knowing who we are
we watch the ghost of us drift
from room to room
through friends and lovers
never quite as real as advertised.

Not saying half we mean
or meaning half we say
we dream ourselves
from birth to birth
seeking some true self.

Until the fever breaks
and the heart can not abide
a moment longer
as the rest of us awakens,
summoned from the dream,
not half caring for anything but love.

I sought myself unsuccessfully

I thought enlightenment was someone
better inside me
But he was nowhere to be found
I called out to him
I bargained and made false promises.

But I could not reach him
because I was sick
so broken of self
I destroyed what I loved
and turned away from that certain Oneness.

I thought surrender was defeat,
to let go was to give up ground.

I was a liar, once a thief, never easy in my mind
yet I longed so to know the origin of the grace
on the lips of those who seem to love so well.

Rumi says something about even the oceans being jealous
of the supplicant's tears. They are the source
of the Ganges and the Amazon. Still frozen in glaciers
prehistoric tears begin to melt the history
of human grief lapping at the base of tall buildings.
Joining with the tears of all the others overflowing
the swollen heart. Long ago they formed the Jordan,
the Ganges, the Jumna from Shiva's top-knot
just as long ago Buddha said the tears
of all our loss could fill the Indian Ocean
and the pond you played in as a child.
The Great Satisfaction followed no satisfaction
we knew, but instead dissatisfaction
until the longing overcame the tendency
to spare too many parts of ourselves.

My skin still burns with the love
I would steal for myself which has not been offered
to that poor soul who hates himself and others
to whom compassion has not been directed,
in whose medulla a round is being chambered.

I become smaller and smaller; disappearing,
people trip over me, my ego is enormous.
But love brings me down gives me shape
allows me to begin again and again.

Trust Your Vision

Trust your vision
    make it whole
    hold it like the Navajo
    his solemn desert oracle
    in quest of shaman passage
    gaining his healing chant
    guiding him through life.

Hold the vision
    constantly rising
it is the way nature works
    through you
it is the only self
    an everchanging underdream
a vision (if you see it)
    up to you
to make real.

Act on your vision
    and pray that you are blessed.

Mother of us all

Mother-of-us-all prays to free us
from our image of perfection
to which so much suffering clings.

When in the shadowy mind
we imagine ourselves imperfectly,
praying to be freed from gravity
by enlightenment, she refines our prayers.

Putting her arms around us
she bids us rest our head on her shoulder
whispering, Don't you know
with all your fear and anger
all you are fit for is love.

Seeing her face this morning I had to send praise

Ananda Ma says, "God comes to us in the guise of suffering."
Crowded 'round are those who wish to fill their heart with her,
"To be close to The Mother is all we want."

She comes in our dreams, sleeping or waking, and tells us she is
as close as a thought. Comes when she is summoned. Lives just
beneath our skin.

Whether we find our true teachers in a momentary glance or a
lifetime of service, in a book or in a cathedral, in a single gatha or a
stupa, in Her eyes or His, it is an initiation greater than birth.

Mother Teresa said she saw the ill and dying as "Jesus in His
distressing disguise." How dedicated the heart must be to catch its
own reflection in another.

In India passing and departing many say "Namaste"
acknowledging the divine in each other.

So many kind personifications, so many reasons to be thankful.

Genuflecting before a great ponderosa, or touching our
forehead to the feet of a gratitude-soaked image of the formless, or
covering our head before the first form, we continue our pilgrimage
into a certain Oneness.

Some see this Oneness in the eyes of their teacher; others catch
a glimpse in a flickering candle or a grain of sand, in a breaking wave
or a tear rolling slowly down a child's cheek. Zen masters note it in
the snap of a twig or the death of their mother.

In our longing is the irresistible draw toward the great satisfaction of devotion. Devotion of greater consequence than any object of devotion.

Step after step, breath after breath, we are able to step within each step, to find the breath within the breath, and within that the sacred essence just where Kabir said we would.

We come as children

We come as children with nursery rhymes of God and birds singing at our bedroom window.

We come as children through years of confusing grace to find what we are looking for is looking back at us, our suffering brings us closer.

Ramakrishna tapped Vivekanada with his toe and spun him through solar systems Jung feared and longed for, and opened to me the first wisdom door I walked through. Now again he calls to me all these years later still living in the book, opening a passageway to the actual.

We come naked at last to the truth, dismayed till the last moment before, then expectant of the inborn gift breaking the horizon . . . oh full moon, oh the surging upward of the heart . . . oh the shining within everything . . . and the gratitude for grace.

We come as children fumbling with our lives, tripping and bruising; for a moment balancing on both feet to find our way through the labyrinth into our inmost dwelling.

From the center we follow the curving upward into space and the settling downward as well, herding the Minotaur across the stellar maze. The oxen fed and stabled with the deer. The singing in the temples bridges the mind. The prayer is everywhere the same.

A drop of pond water

A drop of pond water
under the microscope
just like in science class
but now you are the pond
and the microscope is mindfulness.

ʃ

Wriggling creatures follow the edge
of the world, their world, a world
without an axis, that does not turn
but pulsates rounded like the eye
that observes . . . the convex eye explores
the bend in the cosmos through bent glass
(Is this the wisdom door of "The observed is the observer"?)

Seeking a way out of what imprisons it
and gives it life: the paramecium's quandary.
In the round circus of the drop Medusa furtively
seeks the forgiveness of the unborn. The shores
of amoebic islands continually advance and retract
in the tiny currents that hold their shifting shape.

ʃʃ

Examining up through the microscope the curve of the retina
the razor-fish of fear glisten in the shallows
and dive into the depths to return disguised
as "a practical concern for damnation"
and an unrealistic distrust
in the moon undulating in the waves.

Passing through the retinal screen
wish and dream ride over and slide under
each other, shape-shifting along the long nerve
to the cortex creating the perjury of perception.
Well behind the drawing board telegram-like-impulses
relay the well-edited bundles across synaptic ravines
like salmon jumping waterfalls.
On the specimen slide the whole herd of us
wriggling and whirring. Whirling like moths rising
from flame thoughts flutter up and perish,
no life shorter than a thought's.

Having been born of swamp gas, the surface of the mind
covered in floating duckweed, having condensed from mists
we are all that is left of Creation. The rain that fills the footprint
that pollywogs unsuccessfully inhabit, the trickle that finds the
pond bringing with it all the gritty history of its crossing
open ground, a film of dust disguised as kinetic art
traverses the great waters. Mimicking amoebas
(or Arp's palette) the pond ignores the critics.

We are pond water and a shocking insight about gravity
and fire . . . and the miracle that breathes in unison, rising
from the pulmonary moisture, leaving nothing behind. Our
body made from the drop we are allotted and share with all
That.

Loons in winter

Where do the loons go in winter?
Their resting ground as yet undiscovered,
they migrate into the unknown; passing overhead
they echo in our wild interior, no place assured
for cherubim or heraldic waterbirds;
heading north perhaps following the crease
in the palm, or down our "life line" south,
resting with buddhas and limegreen frogs
between unmapped lily pads. Or following the spirit-fire rising
through the bright tunnel of the spine, maneuvering the canyons
between the eyes, settling unseen amidst the islands rising
from the dark sea behind the brow, raising their plumage
like antennae to the moon's warm wind rustling
night-blooming jasmine through their shining feathers.

As a boy I sat in my canoe on the mirror waters
of Winnipesaukee and watched them slide and drop beneath
the sky plated on the surface.
Looking down through the dark waters to catch a glimpse
of their disappearing, my sight trailing off into shadows
sliding through the dark chasing bass and pickerel
through the slippery bottom-grass.
Rising through striated light to nest on floating thatch.

Hummingbirds migrate 250 miles across the Sea of Cortez
without food or rest on their way to their seasonal home ground.
Monarchs travel thousands of miles to hang like tropical flowers
from their favorite trees. Salmon swim backward as fingerlings
to not be pulled too quickly into the sea and jump waterfalls
when returning to that same hollow in the riverbed
from which they wriggled free from their original eggs.
The blood pumped from our heart to our lungs
and back again follows this same migratory route.

The lightning storms across the surface of the cerebellum presage
monsoons toward the equator, and the freezing and thawing
of streams and lakes to the north, flocks of songbirds
and butterflies follow the double helix home.

And we sit beneath the fire of an autumnal oak on hillsides dying
emerald and gold, trees weeping scarlet leaves, our heart ready
to burst into its next pilgrimage.

And the loons have headed off God knows where.

What does it take

Ghalib says, "The drop of water goes through many difficulties
before it becomes a pearl."

What does it take a drop of water to become a pearl,
how many times back and forth, back and forth,
between the ocean and the clouds?
How many times falling without knowing
where we might land, or how painful
or destructive? How many times
drying on the eye of the dying
or passing through the bowel,
or ruined in the fires
only again to find ourselves
not destroyed after all but only
changed to a new vapor. Light
and shiny. Luminescent mist,
only for a moment able to convince ourselves
it will never rain again.
How many times passing through the oyster?
How many waves broken on the nature of the beach?

Never knowing what part of us is spirit
and what is matter, noting the drop frozen
on a wolf's eyelash, and wet on the eye,
and the fog of winter breath drifting, it wants
to know as solid/liquid/gas which is its true self.
What is real! Who, indeed, am I?

In the tide pools of the lungs
moist anemones open and close
with the incoming waves,
allowing, in the outwash,
life to slip past into the body.

Never certain how to become the treasure
that is sought, the luminous mist penetrates
the iridescent shell, the starry shell, that holds
the ocean of being of which we are composed
and in which we float.

When nothing obscures the darkness
or is blinded by the light
harmony takes its natural form
as a tear. And slowly
crosses the cheek of the world.

The drop of water back and forth
through paradise and hell
loses its slightly metallic taste
and ends its proprietary relationship
with the ocean. It simply becomes
a drop of water.

Once a great Indian musician
who lamented that he had lost his pearl
in a glass of whisky said he would
not sing again until his ruined pearl
would once again become pure as water.

He asked us how might a pearl
become again a drop of water.
He was weeping pearls.

I woke up swimming

I woke up swimming
in the honeycomb of memory
    Looking down into their wells
    flying fish and dolphins reestablish
    the core of the earth.

Manatees and fresh water porpoise
doing flower arrangement upstream,
chrysanthemum petals drifting onto lily pads,
lotus in the cells and along the Nile
in the spine red-eyed lime-green frogs
wait like souls to be born.

Something in me has never awakened fully
from the primal ocean, from the electric sea,
and the rustling in the muscle sheath
that wants so to jump free and swim
like a gray wolf through the evening pines.
Or follow a river of wild ducks and tawny geese,
ease itself into the idle waters,
lift its feet from the streambed
and begin to float—oh how the wolf loves
to float and dream of being a big shiny black beetle
full of shiny eggs that are being laid behind it into the stream,
she dreams of giants and flying dragons hatching
from these black specks . . . eggs born in the East of samurai
and shaven-headed poets spearing drunken fish
with a ceremonial long sword; eggs born in the West
of poets killed sure as Jesus against a sunny wall,
of monks in exquisite parchments, Saint John's whisker

for the eyes and lips, and the beard that kept dreaming
of the second waters that consecrated death before
the skull soft as a flowerbed had a fair chance.
Eggs from the south that floated down the Amazon
from prehistory to Rio de Janeiro, from gar to sea bass,
own the song throat and the lyrics of the torn net
the fish sing upon returning home.
And eggs from the north that come to rest in
the land of the heart and germinate there nurtured
by mantra and prayers, by intention and inclination,
by little words that fill with holy water in a realm
where all water is holy and float me in my sleep.
    I float on a raft of northern eggs downstream
on mountains filled with mendicants and tigers
bowing in the fresh morning air. And from the north
scrolls and tablets, papyrus treatises, secret formula
grown into ancient oaks, dorjes and bells,
heirloom stones with shamanic runes, death poems
left by living treasures from the Cold Mountains,
and the headwaters of the Ganges I float down
in the longboat of my dreams. Gopis and rakshas
scrum on the riverbanks between the burning ghats,
the blue smoke of prayers carried with the departed,
more fully departing. A wisp of smoke from a butter lamp
drifts into the lama's left ear; the prayer wheels turning
at his window are all that keeps his blood flowing
past ancient temples and modern cities, past the saris
and double breasted suits, past pennies for cremation
and lavish weddings, past Bopal and the mother dying,

past paradise and purgatory, into the Indian Ocean
swarming with the eggs of promising legends
and celestial water serpents that soothe the back of our neck
and make a delicious breakfast from our dreams.

I awoke swimming in poems and salamanders
scuttling across the bare floor of waking,
the tiny scythes of their nails tapping
coded images as on a wall between prison cells.

I awake as awareness, then the body and the thoughts that
try to convince us we are alive and well. They seldom succeed.
Perhaps if they did we would not dream or have an ocean nest
hatching thoughts and feelings in the fire body, the water body,
the wind body, the cairn body like a sentinel
on a fog-soaked ocean cliff. I have not lost my gills.

This water I am born into in sleep and waking
carries me again downstream. I am a Buddha's gut
of frog eggs adrift in the stream, each egg a sun
spinning a galaxy, the Milky Way trailing from
the shiny beetle as it waddles across the night sky.
And the world that never leaves the treetops,
that swims awake in the canopy above
the crabs and mollusks of the jungle floor
and the octopi that nest in huge white blossoms.
As the painters of dreaming beasts doze off
floating down the Orinoco and awaken
as a child in a small sailboat on the big lake,
the wind from the north my best friend.

Bubbles crossing the moon

Li Po broke droughts in his dreams.
He knew how to breathe under water,
the death of century-old *koi* like a wave
that passes from his lungs through the heart
and out the top of his head, sweeping, in his case
a few unfinished poems before it as bubbles
crossing the moon.

Swans gradual and sudden

"Spring comes and the grass grows by itself."
                              —*an old Zen assurance*

She wants to know when
the weather will change
or do the seasons lose their impermanence
for another decade?

As an example of winter she says
there is a lake up in the mountains
on which the swans play chess
with the clouds moving across
the mirror. Carp leap from between
the eyes like insights into the gambit
but fish live forever so it is difficult
to know when they are telling
the truth, and which one.
They say "Look after my daughter
while I'm gone" and disappear
taking autumn with them.
Old stories, legends of creation,
won't keep Hades from becoming Paradise.
Rumi said for the person who loves the truth
"their water is fire."
He made spring out of winter,
he learned from his mistakes.
There were moments when numb
from thinking we forgot
we pass through hell
on our way to heaven.

And if the glow has not distracted
us too much, hypnotized at last by peace,
we continue on through Heaven
into the boundless enormity
which dwarfs it.

The swans drink from the mirror
and fly down to fill the rivers
with slippery silver and glistening salmon.

The beating of wings fills the lake
with swans that have flown up
into the mountains bringing
the sky with them.
In the blizzard of their wings
clouds drift out from under
the prayer cloth of long
white flight feathers.

When the swans shrugged their shoulders
and opened their operatic wings
to unfold the star-map
they offered a path, a migration
route really, across the snowscape
of small mind's faint spaciousness.
Drawing us through merciful eyes
into the bigger mind, which has room
for everything and its opposite, paring slowly
until only the One remains
without duality, and becomes the whole it.

The swans of the Eye of Beauty
promise not to give us more
than we can let go of. A long white
wing feather drifts into our dreams.

Oh the upkeep!
Feathers sliding through the machinery
of perception and dreams, following
the same well-worn route, propelled
by the same well-worn "me."

There is something in us,
a separate awareness, in which
we live that experiences clearly
the senses as they roll in before
people with clothes on come
to interpret them, and make
very small sense of the dawn.

Before the swans came
it was a pretty slow news day.

The Earth in Meditation

In a faint indentation worn in the old abbey floor

where a man in robes sat for a hundred years,

the pains of the world burned away

thought by thought feeling by feeling,

swells the ocean of compassion

Chuang Tzu in the meditation hall

Once Chuang Tzu sat next to me in the meditation hall
What a steady breath! And what pale hands,
some might call useless so he just wrote poems
that followed the invisible path of Tao so clearly seen.

A meditation bench creaks, a string of pearls breaks
at 2:00 a.m. and takes at least a century to drop
to the worn stone convent floor still praying
under the meditators. Things change!

Jesus doing walking meditation slowly crosses
a large stained glass window lit from within
by Chuang Tzu's old full moon turning blue
the dimly lit corridor. His feet are light as water.
He is practicing to step away from the boat.

No superstition in the breath

Sometimes when I meditate
there is nothing left of me
but the breath
all the rest of me inseparable
from all the rest of you.

There is no superstition in the breath
only in the mind and body surrounding.

The mind and body are suspicious,
full of fables and myths;
but there is no superstition in the breath.
With each inhalation
With each exhalation
wordless sensation migrates
from the nostrils to the belly and back again
brings water to the fields,
brings breath down the cord from mother to child,
brings blood to the sacrifice of love and war,
brings bright offerings to the temple;
sings into the dark,
assuring the aspirant bent in the shadow
the breath that never ends,
whether dropped to our knees below the cross,
or easy in the slippers of the Beloved,
and certainly behind the diamond brow,
sighs the sigh heard 'round the world.

That famous ten percent we are supposed
to have use of our brain seems true
of the rest of the body and mind as well.
We occupy very little of ourselves
A few percent perhaps . . .

We barely inhabit the breath
living in the shallows of our life.
Our ordinary breath hollowed by fear and anger,
lost behind the nostrils somewhere near the heart,
lost somewhere between the back of the cave
and the top of Jacob's ladder . . . our cells
are starving for breath.

The breath does not lie.
It has nothing to say
It simply is
overflowing with sensation
met crossing the bright field
inviting the body and the rest of the mind
to enter subtle as the breath
subtler levels of being . . .

The fable of each inhalation, like the first
firing of the imagination (full of the superstition of "I")
and animating the body; that first inhalation
still being drawn . . .
And that last exhalation suspended in myth
begun to be expelled soon after birth.

Taking each breath as if it were the last,
before we enter the enormity at the center
of each breath.

Though superstition surrounds the first breath
and is rarely discarded even with the last,
these two breaths—separated by joyful swoons
and plaintive cries—come together in the great silence,
the bitter tears before and after
the great peace between breaths
when mind slows to wisdom and the body
knows itself, as T. S. Eliot nearly says,
for the very first time.

The wise man, the flying woman, dwells
in the space between breaths as faint echoes
drop over the edge and fade into
the vast chasm of silence.

Letting go at the end of each out-breath
stills the enormity.

Occasionally in the meditation hall my breath
nearly stopped. I needed nothing more
as thought stilled, and the wind-blown mind
settled. As the drum stopped.
Breath and fear surrendered.
"If the breath never returns
the universe will breathe for me."

Overcoming the distrust, not holding
to the last breath or grasping at the next.
Letting go completely of control of the breath.
Trusting a breath unshaped by pretense
or superstition, a breath that breathes itself
from the oceanic tides between planets . . .
a breath like the one before
the one that created the universe,
that began thought, and forgot
its original face.

Hatching dragonflies

Sunspots are lily pads,
Buddha a dragonfly.

Remember the first time
your heart froze

it was a hell of a day

but nonetheless
dragonflies were hatching

Nothing realer than the illusion of time

Almost everyone is lost in the fourth dimension. We define ourselves
by memory. We believe in time. We are right for the wrong reasons:
time is as real as we are but no realer. Those coffee spoons in
which Prufrock measured moments of our life are the confluence
of happenstance and inclination.

Schedules and shame. Hope and remorse define us. Escaping from
time into the present, into timelessness, the deeper we go the less
definable we become. And the more real.

When my old teacher lost time I held his watch before him and he
giggled, nothing was as real as the unreality of time. When death
reminds us we do not own time, many more moments are kindly
noticed in their passing.

Caruso reminds me of my childhood. And remembering I remind
him. He clears his throat of childhood and death. Angels and waves
of self-forgiveness wash clear the shore where time meets all that
died despite our love. All we loved despite death.

At one time before they broke the armoring over their belly many
used to say "time is money," as did those who said "time is death."

And what have we learned from the past to enlighten the present,
to bring peace and stop the ten thousand moment to moment wars
waged in the judgmental mind. When we are no longer superior
to anyone or anything mercy leaps from cell to cell and we are set
ablaze with care for all sentient beings. And come to see we too are
one of those sentient beings we have vowed to free from suffering.
We too are made of timeless stuff connected to all else.

What we carry forward is everything we can not let go of.

There is no time but the illusion of time. But we never truly know this until we have disappeared at least a moment into timelessness.

If prayer would do it

If prayer would do it
I'd pray.

If reading esteemed thinkers would do it
I'd be halfway through the Patriarchs.

If discourse would do it
I'd be sitting with His Holiness
every moment he has free.

If contemplation would do it
I'd have translated the Periodic Table
to hermit poems, converting
matter to spirit.

If even fighting would do it
I'd already be a blackbelt.

If anything other than love could do it
I've done it already
and left the hardest for last.

When we are cured

The donkey thinks it's too far to walk
but walks none-the-less.
The goat cart carries the ancestors
with the slavery-ending sword
and the honing wheel.
The deer cart for the tongueless Buddhas,
who are known by their being.
The bullock cart for the Bodhisattvas
and their love children waiting
to be born.

Though we sit alone beneath the banyan
many have shown us the way.

Having brayed of Buddhas and doctrines
the wide larynx becomes a narrow ledge
on the climb past footholds and feet.

To make it easy for the rocky mind
we say "illumination" and "vastness"
but there is no path when we are cured
of gravity and the idea of the body.

To live inside our life

To live inside our life, with the senses fully exposed
seeing smelling feeling from day to day
the world growing close, then fading,
trying to find a way to pull the long blue molecules
of the sky within, perhaps mining our bones
for prehistory, seeking our source,
might for a season quell the longing,
but there is in the hollow of our bones
gain and loss and the smell of cordite
in death's war garden . . .
there is one precious moment
and it's all passed beyond us without stopping.

Standing still

He is standing still after a lifetime
of movement. He has built a hut
under a tall pine beside a seasonal creek.
Without rain the stones are silent.
The western wind keeps up the pace.
A rush of thought fills the stream-bed
and changes the conversation
at a thousand polished dinner tables.

When human beings meditate

When human beings meditate
they sometimes close their eyes
and feel this body—
a flickering field of sensation
a tingling, hot and cold,
gravity here and there.

And attend to the breath
at the belly or nostrils
choose one
and stay there five years—

not the thought of the breath
but the sensations accompanying
each inhalation, each
exhalation. The beginning
the middle and the end
of each in-breath
and the space between
where thinking wriggles free.

The beginning
middle
and end
of each out-breath

and the space between
and thought
and the space between thoughts—

returning to the breath—
just sensation breathing itself,
sensations sensing themselves
floating in space. Even some idea of who
is doing all this
floats by.
Just another bubble.

Another thought thinking itself all by itself
the fragile moment
vanishing in space

returning to the breath
like a devotee to a vow.

Watching thoughts
think themselves,
unfolding one into the next—
existing only a moment
before dissolving, watched
frame by frame in the passing show,
even such notions as impermanence
passing in the flow.

Observing feelings arise uninvited—
pleasure and pain, desire and
disappointment, liking and disliking
all day long from thought

to thought, a surprisingly mechanical
process unfolds.
Watching consciousness dream world
after world, self after self, constantly pretending
someone to be, arising and dissolving
quicker than advertised, unconvinced
we really exist.

Sinking into the light of awareness
that floods consciousness and sees
what we are looking for is
what is looking.

The breath breathing itself,
thoughts thinking themselves
feelings feeling themselves,
moment to moment unfolding.

When human beings meditate
they sometimes close their eyes
and enter their body with mercy
and awareness—follow their thought
to its source, noting the pressure
at the base of the spine
and the fountain in the skull.

Sometimes when we meditate
nothing special occurs
for the very first time.

Reading Rilke . . . for Allen

His words drop through
a Milky Way of neurons
and reaching appropriate quadrants
explode

I am surprised at how well
he knows me, and challenges me
to a duel just to see. He tempts
lobotomy for uncovering what
can really be said.

Cantoists all
Allen approving the Oracle mock-ups
with a long feather drooping from his wing
showed how our caves connected
how fire might find its course
given wholly its chance.

Cartoon holy men and hip-handed angels
come to see who is on the watchtower
from which to signal the approach of
the penetrating Light. Double-stringed harps
and tight guitars push the edge of reason.

Sitting in a tree in Golden Gate Park
nesting with my saints and hooligans
planning the death of pride, but this time
burying the body too in the heart
instead of letting it run about bragging.

Sometimes sitting on his boulder in the piney woods
I thank him.
Sometimes standing beside her ponderosa
I nod in agreement.
Sometimes walking down his road
I am suffused with appreciation.
Sometimes remembering that much love
I take a whole breath.

I say

I say cornucopia when I mean horn of plenty

I say compassion when I mean mercy at the fingertips

I say irrational when I mean seeing around corners

I say mountain when I mean bighorn sheep

I say mindstuff when I mean emotional bleeding

I say caring, I say lover, when I mean a green canoe

I say forest when I mean a warm hearth

I say leave the door open when I mean don't forget
  dry socks for the pilgrimage

I say Mediterranean when I mean the fruits of sweet palms

I say mines dug straight into the South American caliche,
  when I mean slavery

I say slavery when I mean the gold coins and broken bracelets
  of charmed women

I say cause and effect when I mean pleasure and pain

I say pleasure and pain when I mean love and hate

I say barrel of a gun when I mean a barrel of a gun

I say bullet when I mean a numb shoulder

I say peace when I mean dried blood

I say kindness when I mean the Buddha

I say the Buddha when I mean the peaceful child

I say mercy when I mean the other child

I say the Salton Sea when I mean inland kisses

I say Spring when I mean haiku

We stop counting syllables when there are no fingers left

in meditation, and the world has begun without us

I say end when I mean something very different
even if I do not quite know what it is.
I say love when no other word will do.

Slick Willy's metaphysics

Lying he nonetheless told the truth

When asked if death and life are the same or different

he said it all depends on what your definition of "is" is.

The Salad

Sometimes I use platitudes instead
of nasturtium flowers in the salad,
the colors like stepping-stones across
the delicate jungle in the old Chinese bowl
whose crane's wings lift
ever so slightly the porcelain centuries
from the black birch table.

There are truths among the frilly lettuce
and the slick tomatoes; even the adzuki bean
has its point of view. The truth apparently
was born into the salad. Or maybe
it was there in the bowl before we started.

Somehow a pebble has found its way
from Hari's shack in the Kush to the shiny
bottom of my dish. It is like one
of those pinnacle islands that jut
from the China Sea.
A bit of black olive like a beached whale
—having traveled a thousand miles
to drop into this bowl—
lies exhausted against the stone island.

Again Machado asking for "a few honest words"
mixing the tart with the sweet, the ruby vinegar,
sharp as a new knife and the first pressings
of the golden olive tree. And perhaps, just perhaps,

if we are truly hungry, Eve's apple pie of knowledge
and fearlessness to fill Adam, who had never eaten,
waiting in our bones to take birth in Eden. And
Adam with that apple in hand taught geography
to each son and split the world into the hemispheres
of the brain which only love can cross and war can
never win, straightened Vulcan's crippled leg
in hopes the fires of war would cool and the anvil turn
to an herbal cure.

        The gods are aging, their developmental disorder
which has long kept them at arm's length
is beginning to predominate and has left them
terribly lonely and a bit late at answering prayer;
there are some from Agamemnon and Orpheus
still on their plate. They no longer write poems
to keep clear the passageway between the heart
and mind. There seems an old age preoccupation
with matters of safe passage.

        Diamonds in the lettuce. Emeralds in the eyes.
The Crown Jewel of Liberation instead of a gold sovereign
on the porcelain lids of death. The Precious Gem,
tossed with the greens, stirred by the wild horses
crossing the dewy meadow just below a red dawn
rising to the lip of the bowl.

The best truth remaining the pebble before we name it.

J knew a man who stopped breathing

I knew a man who stopped breathing
for forty years. He was like a honeycomb
in whose pockets children liked to rummage
for treasure. When he told them of golden *amrit*
rivers touching the surface where purity sits,
where love remains after all, the children
stopped breathing and began to glow
like a summer evening. Gradually every one
took the same breath. Lifted
into similar heavens and giggled
when the breath returned tickling
the rim of their nostrils. But he had
given away the world long ago
in exchange for everything.
He knew a bargain when he saw one.
He was open at both ends
and there was a humming in his chest,
a page from the songbook of the wind . . .

Sometimes we can't wait

Sometimes we just can't wait for the moon
to set, for the stars to remain just a moment
longer. Sometimes we just can't wait for birth,
can't wait for death. Can't wait for the body
to wriggle free of itself when pain
runs the long bones of our inescapable future.
They are already preparing the earth for
our arrival.
Alert the microbes and the earthworms
as they eat their way through
that eternity resides in my heart
that they should digest thoroughly and
close their mouths while chewing
lest a poem is lost. Remind the worms
we long to pass through the length
of them and return to soil.

Put your ear to the ground and listen
to the song of the earthworms tending
the shrine of my corpse, taking Eucharist
from my delicious thumb.

SECTION 3

Devotion in the Air Element

When we begin to breathe through
our gills sometimes we catch our breath
serenely leaving town without us,
gone fishin' for the Big One
using our soul for bait.

Two predominant currents flow in humankind above the din
of war: the *mind stream* of undifferentiated clarity, and the endless
nectar of the *heart stream.*

Some strong presence of the Beloved is acknowledged in almost
every devotional practice, just as the fruits of mindfulness are
honored in even differing Buddhist sects.

Sitting on my cushion in "a Buddhist manner" for decades with
every doubt and blessing passing through without a quaver or a
kriya (involuntary movement due to the breaking loose of spiritual
energy) sometimes when I chanted for an evening with old friends
from the Hindu *sangha* with whom I share a Great Teacher,
my body often began to shake and the words began to shimmer.
Ram Jai Ram Jai Jai Ram. His song comes true.

Called beyond my edge the words become like pearls floating
in air. The dark tunnel of the throat, the bright passageway through
which the dying access the rest of their life filling with images of
the yet unborn, meadows and temples just behind the brow.

The words offer handhold after handhold as I climb.

Grace in every breath.

The light has been left on for us

I watch my thoughts, my actions, and
find it hard to believe that's me!

I hear my words and wonder who
is speaking and who does he
think he is!

I am the imaginary hero of my hopes
lost between verbs that require I know
who I am, but I am just a passing thought—
yet somehow, somehow—as close to a
miracle as we get—the nature
of the heart—the Beloved
has left the light on for us all night . . .

God does not answer prayer

God does not answer prayer.
It is a sacrilege to think so.
An insult to the god-drenched hearts
of all who pray through the night
and in the morning are nonetheless
handed a dead child.

The churches in Salem used to burn heretics
to increase attendance. Now those who feel
their prayer didn't reach quite far enough,
that they were not pure enough,
are victims of a merciless atheism
that says all good fortune comes from God
though the brutal often prosper
and it is not uncommon to torture
the pure of heart.

We pray for the best, forgetting
the unpredictable unfolding
that must occur for us to learn
prayer for others works better
than for ourselves. Jesus prays
in the garden of Gethsemane
and is refused. Ten thousand,
ten million prayers rise in Latin,
Arabic, Hindi, and Hebrew

yet their husbands and wives,

children and sisters, fathers and brothers

do not survive well if at all

though in their chest beats strong the sacred heart.

No prayers are granted, none denied.

True prayer reaches well beyond the edge of the world.

It enters head bowed into the arms of the Beloved.

Impatient with grace, we pray faster

Some see grace as their destination,
others as their process. Both however
often share the trap of wanting
to "go faster than grace."

Born into a life in which we own nothing
yet love none-the-less,
we become attached to so much
then decompose when what we never owned
departs.

Though we may be hard in sorrow,
unable to discern our face in the mirror,
pained as we may be, that does not alter
the fact that behind who we think we see
grace is our original face.

Grace comes in many guises:
The Heyoka rides backwards
to see what's coming.
Owl-eyed salmon hatchlings
swim tail-first to slow the current
and plot from grace as from the stars
a course toward Mother Ocean.

Grace makes no excuses.
It says it takes courage to be moral,
that compassion is fearlessness.

What the Buddha had to confront on his way into grace
was not just lust and fear but his attachment
to sorrow and beauty.

Not knowing

I may not know my original face
but I know how to smile.
I may not know the recipe for the diameter
of a circle but I know how to cut a slice
for a friend. I may not be Mary or the Buddha
but I can be kind. I may not be a diamond
cutter but I still long for rays of light
that reach the heart.
I may not be standing on the hill of skulls
but I know love when I see it.

Many have gone mad

Many have gone mad looking for a solid center,
but there is none.
We think of centering as only a continual narrowing
of focus until we touch the pearl
but in practice it is often a continual expansion
of focus until we become the ocean.

Our center is vast space, boundless awareness
indistinguishable from unconditional love.

Of course I play the fool when I dare allow
consciousness to describe itself! Isn't that the birth
of the ego, the "I am this" that closed behind us
when we entered the body?

The Beloved on the mountainside

Snow here last night at 7200 feet
and in the morning footprints
of the Beloved circumambulate the house,
the snow littered with mantra and song,
almost too much delight to step out from old quarters
to stand *tumo* burning in the melting snow,
the songs and prayers melting, nothing to hold on to.

Mirabai writes that to know the Beloved, to be the Beloved,
we must be willing to "cut off our head and sit on it."
But the head's not worth what it used to be,
got a bunch of holes in it and a big one on top.
A Jack-o'-lantern lit from within by a longing for grace.

Even the teacher's blessing kept in our pocket
can be an obstruction to the enormity of Being,
but better yet no Being, just a little being at a time,
no sideways glances, no idea of how to do it,
and with verse close on our heels, we can't find a noun
that tells the truth or a verb that is not bragging.

For Lee's Toe 1939–2007

Listening to Caruso I touch my forehead to your feet.
My feet too listen, one imbalance and another set them too afire,
make me think of Jesus washing their feet in his heart.
I've tried that, softening and sending love,
washing over them with a different kindness,
making big mercy for my feet
but I still take the two factory-coated medications.

Caruso sings of old Pagliacci weeping rivers
I think he's crying because he's wearing clown shoes
I do that sometimes when I don't stand in truth,
my feet turn away from the path, whatever path
seemed once to lead where I was going.
There is something stuck between my toes
I am playing Michelangelo-footsie with the sacred
I am singing to my feet, oh they want so much!
They want to walk through time, stand lightly
before the Delphic Oracle or climb
to the stone tower *gompa* above the mountain pass.

Caruso has turned the aria over to Aretha
her song anoints our feet and floods the spine.

Dispatches from the front

When told that grace is our original face
and the Beloved our true body
the "ripe buffoon" breaks through
and dances with those who reject their foolishness.
He is trying to help. But only the wandering minstrel
and the dervishing chimney-sweep can be trusted.
Only mercy. Only the god-drunken who are ruined
for life and can't help but love.
Only Dionysius and the lotus.

In the dark room he called out uncertainly,
"Bark twice if you are God!"

This awkward speck of dust

This awkward speck of dust,
this universe, time, and every
act and thought
from mineral to man,
deposited in the library of my marrow.

I do not know what I know
it enters through another door,
disturbs my fragile understandings,
rattles my dinnerware and knocks
all my trophies off their shelves.

Breathed in loving madness,
revealed beyond the mind
and the shape of things.

Do not be betrayed
by philosophies and enlightenments—
all there is to be
was yours before you began.

A pinched nerve

A pinched nerve
    at the root of the fingers
tried to pick up
    more than it could handle
but in the pain
    without reserve or wish
to be otherwise
    the Light,
Ah there! Christ in the palm of your hand.

The devotional dilemma . . . for M.

He betrayed me, that two-faced traitor,
He tossed my prayers aside, He lied to me
He told me I would be protected,
"Just call out my name!"
but suffering migrates through my days.

Still the toxins unresolved by birth
enclose me like a shroud.
I am abandoned near-by.

He whispered behind my back
and made me distrust God, guru, and self.

He pissed me off so much I tore down all his pictures
and took his name out of my poems.
I stuck his likeness in a drawer
to save the frames "for something better."
I threw away all his photos and was glad of it.

But there was one
that pulled at my heart
and I could not put it aside
it made me want to cry for joy
that he is in my life.

Ondrea in her smooth skin

ʃ

She said in her smooth skin
You know we are just a wild thought
not just you and me
but mankind and unkind—
>   *just behind her and to the left a snowy owl*
>   *opens sky-filled wings—*
>   *clouds drift in feathery down,*
>   *meteor showers from the scapula*
>   *to the wingtips, stars in the hollow bones.*

Just beneath her skin an old Greek cipher that uncapped
the hidden "I," freeing a handful of comets in the skull
that drop into their appropriate Delphic dreams
that are not dreams at all, some of the few
that care about the poems in people.

Some poems draw the unkind poison from our seeing
hold it dearly stepping over the edge
falling off the end of a long kind line . . .
>   *a warm white wind tips the urn spilling music*
>   *onto palette or page, draws it across the strings*
>   *as one molecule at a time polishes*
>   *the fine edge of a favorite chisel*

Some people paint with camel hair brushes,
some cover their fingers in colors to honor the gods,
some are children some are priests,
some take more than they give, selfish art
shouts ungodly from a doorway as we pass.

Some people are as kind as music,
some wait 'til death has left the room
to stop posing, they are like anemic
string quartets played by separate
instruments from separate rooms.

The wild thought that catalyzed the formless
into something to be, a toaster or a Buddha,
Sariputra or fire hydrant, an ant with one short leg
leaving runic footprints between sun-filled grains
of sand, no more than a wild thought, a passing shadow,
to the stones she crosses or perhaps she remained a dream
in the starry maze under the snowy wing.

We are a passing thought that leaves
little the same for even a mind-moment.
In the shadow cast by thought
one slides across another
into the light that streams through the retina,
past the branching nerves and the worn dance floor,
past monks unmoving by the path to steady
our way and haiku here and there calling
like hidden treasure from under a rock
and drop into the lap of the woman holding her lover's hand
in her smooth skin complete with wild thoughts.

II

Moving from body to body
from phylum to phylum
up the ladder of the species
following Ulysses far and back
past searchlights and car alarms
and *The Origin of the Species* in Basho's
backpack next to an old map and a patch of bad weather,
following the old alphabet home vertebra by
vertebra, genus by genus, up the serpent
into the skull—"bowl of stars" already a cliché
in just a few lines—so no bowl empty or full,
but instead the shaman's rattle and that wild thought
continuing upward through the top of the head
out into the silver universe . . .

III

She said sometimes the wind creates life
from the foam on a green wave,
each shiny bubble a green cell,
an egg, a scanning eye, a turning wheel,
each turning toward what the Greek poets
called Paradise, the Elysian Fields,
but sometimes for the longing
even heaven is too small.

The one who stands by the door
with bags packed says that won't do,
that Paradise is only pleasure, not enough
to keep the ball rolling one more turn
to invent the wheel again circling Mount Kailas,
crossing the crevasse between hemispheres
returning again into the smooth skin
that guides the body as if it were as real
as thought-things seem.

There is a silence between breaths

There is a silence between breaths
when the heart becomes a sacred flame
and the belly uncoils which reminds me
how remarkable it is to wake
beside you another day.

Between deaths we dreamed together
between breaths, in that stillness,
which has joined us ever since.

In that first breath
we step onto the dance floor,
and waltz unnoticed through the void.
The sacred everywhere we turn
and turn again, as form so generously dissolves
and only the Beloved remains.

In this moment which lasts a lifetime
there is nowhere to stand
where you are not beside me
where you do not accompany me within.

Aswirl in Maya

Om tara, tu tara, ture swaha

Anklets dance the women's feet
fill and empty the perfect vacuum
from one side of the universe to the other,
birthing and deathing
the fruitful emptiness.

The song no longer dormant,
like whales sounding between cells,
leaps the synaptic void,
through the ring of fire in each breath
into the tonal ocean.

Toward the end of birth and death
each imagines what lies ahead.
Listening one may hear creation
tilling the ground . . . the shiny edge
turning the dark soil,
life aswirl in the cosmos.

Dropping through an ocean of neurons
mind moments swim lotus-stemmed channels
imagining who we might be,
an ocean imagining itself a starfish.

Dancing forever, how long it is impossible to say,
the feet still red from birth.

In the midst of a long poem I lose the thread

In the midst of a long poem I lose
the thread that leads back out of the dream.
Where the Beloved so beautifully stood
there is only naked awareness, bright and formless,
before it combines with something smaller
to become consciousness: the womb that births
God and the Beloved, as well as post mistresses
and ink wells, fish fins, causeways, and cathedrals,
and this dream interrupted by grace
from which I awaken like an empty church.

The altar and statuary are gone
only a few stained-glass windows
toss metallic greens and reds on the
gray granite floor, love stories;
the pews are stacked with fluttering wings.

But behind the brow
in the room without walls
we find the reliquary of the collective soul.

I open my eyes to find my bones
turned to charcoal
in an ancient Chinese *sumi* painting.
My bones insist, my eyes too, that
they are made only of consciousness
like everything else, the effect of the same
luminous substance

The warlords have killed God in His name . . .
for G.W.

It is difficult to recognize the face
of the angel of destruction though
his signature in the blood of
the moment is familiar.

Thinking themselves secret agents
for God, following their coughing horse
across the Pacific, untying prophesy
and Tibet, a dynasty of crows
pecks the bones of victory.
The gray smoke of disease
slips into their bodies
between unsafe dreams.

One must beware of their bones
turning to tin on city streets
choked with the invisible catalyst of fear.

Now the sun refuses to come out
from behind steel clouds.
And the moon! Well the moon
no longer shows up on the charts.
It has died most unhappily from
neglect and the quick hot breath
that has "no time for imitations."

Sancho has left Quixote
Mary has left Jesus
Ananda has left Buddha
The panther, worse than death, has left Lorca.

Lazarus shook off death when he heard a friend's voice
Krishna left Vishnu in the movies
Mother has left the nuns to Kali
Katagiri left peace up to warlords
The 14th left the 13th to become invisible
    at last.

Whether it is the blue piecrust tile roof or a map
of Burlingame the light can be seen through
painted plaster walls and frozen waterfalls
growing from the cliff like Easter Island.

Milarepa green without envy for dream-dulling foods
sat in the ice his cotton garment worn away through
a dozen years of meditation and a thousand years
of heat from the magma in his bones;
his marrow white as a star.

Milarepa has not left the cave
A hidden yogin trims the mistletoe
from the weary oak miserable with history,
he also trims the likes of us, he is
the *dorje* mindstream of a much different
angel, crimson and gold—good hats.

Jesus has not left the hill.
We berate ourselves for not knowing
how long will it take us
to get him off the cross?

Sariputra is still at his dying mother's side
and still the celestials are gathering
to attend her ascent.
He will not leave her alone in the world.

Bonnie won't leave Clyde because
he promised her she could die.

The demon Ravanna won't leave Rama
because he wants "only to be killed
by God."

Meister Eckhart won't abandon his Jesus
     even in hell.

The warlords have killed God in His name.

The idiot of sanity

The idiot of sanity rambles
down the street
and sits on my doorstep.

Who invited he wonders the natural catastrophe
of small unethical acts repeated
for generations, he is bored
and sad at having this role.

Last life he was Cleopatra or Brutus
he never can remember which
and both seem present,
he betrays himself daily.

Once he had a bottle of bright blue
pills that changed the color of his eyes
and straightened his limbs
but he got weary of being so small
and left sanity to those who knew best
what to do with it.

When the hidden beauty was revealed to him
he knew if he spoke of it trouble would come
like an eel out of its den
and tear his new shoes, and stop him
from dreaming more that blue.
He knew the sky within the sky,
the breath within the breath,
that the shining cloud had confided.

He felt better not having to pretend
he was sane and became indistinguishable
from love even at the long table of the mind
where recently he was rewarded
with an unending openness of heart.

He seldom quite knows where he is
but he is never lost.

An Angus piece . . .

When even "the only truth" becomes surreal

On the scroll the surrealist dharma poet
called "the history of my spine"
we coincide in the Century of Unknowing
working our way toward the center
from either end.

Dead all these years how foolish
to think he had not slipped
back between the pages
between the breaths, between words.

It made too much sense.
He said, "If it makes too much sense
it's a well-fashioned lie."
He said "sense" is a lesser sensibility,
a lower order of reality.
Small mind. Only what can be
held in our small hands,
the light piling thick as snow on the shoulder,
knee deep in the silver river wild wisdom and
mercy abound.

Where meditations once inhabited heaven & hell
he reminds us to examine the fish that swim
by midnight light suspended by belief
that what is below is above.
They float in the middle way.

Mountains rise to meet the pilgrim's step
and haiku grass grows no matter who you
think you are or where you imagine you live.
Too much sense and too little habitual kindness.
A distinct need for unreasonable mercy.

If you make too much sense you are probably lying
and know it, trying to fit the whole truth
filled with midnight fish into small soft hands,
shiny fish-gut overflowing with slippery verbs
that spill onto the dinner table
like a Dali painting or the hoof-prints of Guernica.

One fish attempts to own us saying *escape*
another owning nothing says *be still and know;*
we lose our appetite for the body,
dive to the bottom of the stream
make a small nest of pebbles and lay our eggs.

Poems hatch where raccoons stride the riverbank
at midnight looking for just such a snack.
But the poems elude destruction by appearing safe
and not making too much sense.

Sometimes the serpent that has worked its way
into the pen can't wait for "between the eyes"
or "the top of the head" and lets both lovely rivers
and flesh hanging from a tree find their rightful
places in Creation that accepts these poems
in lieu of life.

On the scroll the beginning is catching up
with the end. The year's floating the words
of days off the papyrus of memory.

On the dead page living things crawl to the edge
and peer over from the ridge of the circus tent,
they bless the trucked-away tree and wet our fingertips
to turn the dry page that bursts from the binding
held only by faint realities scribbled on what was
a good deal more real. Chopin bleached the tusks
of elephants with slow sensible nocturnes.
Even what passes for surreal these days
seems a bit too well ordered,
too sensible, to swim off the canvas
and give birth in the pebble nest in the diamond stream.

There is an elemental love

There is an elemental love in the universe
by which name we know each other
and encourage ourselves to live.

There is a silver river that connects everything
from which some part of us never leaves.

There is a mercy making its way
up through the ocean of the earth
to the shores of our feet.

There is a music so sweet it is almost unbearable
that is composed between the ear
and the heart which reminds us.

There is a diamond-glint, a seed of longing
in ourselves that recognizes the potential
absence of gravity in another.

There is part of us that
says it is never too late to be reborn
on the inbreath each morning.

Somewhere there is a basket
that contains all our failures.
It is a big basket. It wants to know
what to do with these.
Mercy has no use for them.

Dying into Life and Death

*Chris and I used to sit on his bed and listen
to string quartets when he was dying. He loved
that tattered old "Grateful Dead" tee shirt, it was
so threadbare you could see Auschwitz through it.
Sometimes it's hard to tell whether death is decep-
tive or revealing. It's easy sometimes to mistake the
person in that bed for Jesus. Or the Divine Mother
in her distressing disguise. Sometimes momentarily
radiant with death you see the dying leave. More
often you just feel something move in your heart.*

You'd think we'd be used to it by now

You'd think we'd be used to it by now
dying that is!
But each time at first it seems a little different,
depending on the loneliness or love
from which we push off—how sturdy the boat,
how flat the sea—the style of departure
and the time it takes to make the leap
to surrender our suffering.

How quickly we slip away, still red from birth,
or old and ashy on the porch, still cold
and rocking, "can't let go of living
just used to it by now you know"—
or a cold wet wind that rots us on
the battlefield or at a loss for words headless
from the royal axe, or cloaked in the darkening shadow
of despair in a suicidal corner, the outbreath longer
than in, dead long before death takes us.

How many breaths are we promised?
Are they predetermined like the
number of eggs already present
in that hatchling girlchild's tiny ovaries?

You would think we'd be accustomed to it by now
but dying is one of those things it takes a while
to get used to. And then you find
it's more frightening to take birth.

People keep bringing me their dead

Ululations!

There are ululations at the gate:
with heads tilted back
pleading to an empty sky
clouds devour their prayers.
Those, bodiless, who no longer suffer
are in pain just watching

Emptying the tombs
within a piece of amber placed
on a gravestone one can see nightmares,
kundalini-struggles in the tar pits of the Id,
the labors of the odyssey, the dead in our arms

All that remains is a fossil
of what was bursts of fire and frost,
of creation before it became a myth

The grieving keep bringing me their dead
to pray for.

There are ululations at the inner ear:
a friend with her leg removed by cancer
waiting at the gate

a son casually shot at 18

another long in leukemia

and one who killed himself
in the orchard behind the house

and one who rolled her new white mustang
on graduation night

and one who could not stand on feet
once swaddled in feather slippers can dance again,
who long in the arms of the Divine,
burned clear by illness,
light streaming from his heart,
proposes his kaposi are "hickies from God"

Some with their dead draped like the *Pieta*
across their frozen laps, some are angry,
most living and dead alike have nothing to say
their eyes say it all, ululations turn the retina
dark as amber, but some turn to gold for love
of a neighbor.

Throughout the day they come
to teach me how to pray
on their behalf

My prayers are in the silence
between breaths

Poetry rises like something overheard in a dream,
prayers rise from stanza to stanza,
from phrase to phrase,
connected by the great nothing
at the end of each line

Prayers sent from heart to heart
across the great nothing/big bang
in the palm of Michelangelo's invisible
angel of death leap the space
between God and Adam's fingertips
and land in the back of our mind.

In the realm of the passing away

This is the realm of the passing away. All that
exists does not for long.

Whatever comes into this world never stops sliding
toward the edge of eternity.

Form arises from formlessness and passes back,
arising and dissolving in a few dance steps between
creation and destruction.

We are born passing away.

Seedlings and deadfall all face forward.

Earthworms eat what remains.

*We sing not for that which dies but for that which
never does.*

A different death

The song fills the body
going down through the soles
to connect into the earth.
Songs from the crown of the head
and the soles of the feet
are equally authentic.

Tuning up it says:
We are all carrying the maximum load
allowable by Law. Everyone is burning at the edge
and beyond, so the unexplored
may be illuminated.

What a terrible delight the truth is.
Neither ecstasy nor suicide can reach it.
It destroys only what seemed real.
It destroys all that suffers.
It displays the perfect justice of boundless space.

Truly naked beneath this worn old body,
embarrassed by the trappings of flesh and word
I bow again and again
hoping to catch a glimpse
of grace on the rise.

In the cemetery

Sitting quietly in the cemetery waiting for nothing
the blanket of her knowing is about her,
and the quiet is enough.
The silence draws her into the earth where deep all
tears repose. Seas greater than the Indian Ocean,
Buddha said, wept for all those we have lost.
She cries for love. The mirror for her heart is broken.
Her blood a purple Tao beneath her skin.
Her lungs an ocean of birth and death.
Tears held back too long flow down
the cord from mother to child.
She weeps now so her daughters might be free.

Years later as her life force disengaged from the body
her memories gathered in her heart.
Dissolving into the Ocean of Being she found
a reflecting pool as clear as she had ever known.
Not disappointed by the absence of angels
she died more quietly than expected.
And less dead for it all than even God had promised.
Tilting her head slightly to one side she saw Paradise
in the space between thoughts.

PETER AND TIM

Peter said,
My prayers don't work anymore!
He and Tim had the virus.
Both were ill for years.

In the hospital, then home a while,
then back again. Sometimes
too sick and frightened to visit.

Lovers taking turns dying

Up most of the night and most of the day,
attending to each other. Measuring medications,
applying infusions. Dragging fevers
to midnight emergency rooms.
Sometimes bedpans, sometimes too much
pain in the mind / in the body / in the heart
to have made it one more day alone.

It's said that if you truly love someone
you might well wish they died first.
So great is your concern for their smooth passage
that you are willing to go it alone at the end
just so they won't have to.

When I asked Tim,
What will you do if Peter doesn't come home this time?
he said, Die at last.

Peter died at noon on Sunday.

Passing through my heart on his way elsewhere,
he whispered,
    "It feels so great to be alive again!
        I was so sick for so long."

TIM AND PETER

Tim's mom called this morning.
Looks like it's the end.
Please keep him in your prayers.

The gardener was dying on the first day of spring.
His beloved partner gone on two months before him
to prepare the ground,
so he would have to bring only seeds.

In each diminishing breath violets and chrysanthemums.
A great flowering vine growing from his heart
Up through the top of his head,
like Jack's beanstalk, stretching all the way to Heaven,
emerging into an enormous garden,
    his garden,
        Peter lazy by the fountain.

Sunday poem

Any poem could be the best
Any day the best or worst
A few butterflies in the garden or
the screech of brakes. Not a breath
returns, not a blink of the eye, no
reminiscent smell or bright pebble.

Life comes
And goes.
It's that short.

Just back from the nursery

Just back from the nursery
Working in the garden
So full of life
I forgot death.
But I was planting late
And she reminded me
Winter was coming.

Jennifer on her twelfth birthday

Part of our work was with terminally ill children

A piece of cake with one pink candle
left by the nurses on her nightstand.
Christ crucified to the wall above.

Her childhood consumed by leukemia
she released the future.
And with that last breath
lifted her Jesus from the cross.

Free now to ride her beloved horse.

Sitting beside her empty bed
I sense ancient Mary, Mother of Mercy,
come to cradle the newly dead in her broad arms.
And the children come slowly to the table
for the supper promised from Golgotha.

And I wonder all-too-rational and broken-hearted
how when thousands have died this day
just one Mary can embrace them all.

Offering me her shoulder she whispers:
"When a thousand people look at the moon
there are a thousand moons."

Neruda writes about death

The old poet writes about the silence of death.
He has heard the silence of corpses
hung over battlements. I have heard
many times the same silence differently
from beside what had been clean beds.

But naturally most go deaf with their loved one's
last breath *and miss the whoosh of the light escaping,*
trip and fall between one small bone
and another, slip through the trembling ocean
into the skull, the world broken in the fissured shell,
the light pouring through the inner ear . . .

I have met some deaths with prayers, others with relief,
and of course the silence that steals the tongue
and sets the mind ablaze, the silence like a fragrance
that once breathed bedside always remembers,
whether the rasping struggle
or the quiet hiss of quick release
into the white room,
or the burning battle trench,
or slumped across the dinner table,
or too dead for breakfast . . .
A silence we never forget.

Somehow aging thickens the clouds

The rivers in the fingers are
beginning to freeze over.
Scree along the knuckles.
The fissured face on the rock wall
sadly becomes more discernible.

Neruda to test his sword did homework
for God about salt and a favorite
pair of warm socks. They were
muscular and exquisite. Perhaps
I can give as much praise to my
slow morning.

Ghalib with one eye open
threatens God with the grief
of opening the other, and seeing
beyond, to destroy the throne.
He laughs when the red fox says stop!
Step back! the Beloved will be homeless!
As if his blue tile roof was not long ago
traded for golden thatch. As if it mattered!

No longer defined by our pain
there is no compromise with confusion.
White streaks and grey thickets
hide the hunter in the bone,
the years crouch in wait, eat blessed
food sequestered in our prehistory,
left for us as Paul might say
"by an earlier version of ourselves."

All our marrow exposed on Vulture Peak,
the birds use the calcium
to shine their ebony beaks.

Nerve and living bone cairn the valley floor.
tumbling like a poem becoming unstacked
unruly words hopscotch into phrases, leap
into moment to moment *bardos* changing
with a misplaced verb along the central nerve.

Yet the magma remains within.
When a poem, a breath, a song,
has finished writing the hand
still falls in love with the pen
and will not open,
the fingers fixed around
the airway in the palm.

Blue rivers run down the back
of my arm and whitewater
through the carpal rapids at the bend
of the wrist, then drop over the edge
from one realm to another
where pain is met by love instead of fear
by compassion rather than self-pity.

I knew a man who said he could turn pain into sound.
He was not a musician but more like one of those
19th century surveyors who saw the American West
before the blood killed the grass. Who
named new species but could protect none.
Audubon actually killed everything he painted.
This fellow said he could hear best where
the muscle attaches to the bone. He said
there are overhanging ledges and caves
there in which monks and hermits practice
compassion for all sentient beings;
and if we listen closely to their singing
the hardness might relent and open away the pain
of time folding in on itself.

If suffering made a sound the atmosphere
would be humming all the time
so I asked him, "If you can turn your pain
to sound how come you're not always singing?"
He said, "Because I don't want to frighten people;
it is the same song you hear when you approach death."

Sadness

There is a sadness
That once it enters
Our young lives
Never really departs . . .

A dead bird,
A lost friend.
Our mother crying.

The darkness in the body casts shadows
beneath the stairs
where we learned to pray
all by ourselves.

Sorrow, unattended, accumulates like a stalactite
in the interior of each thought and feeling,
in the darkness the ancestors remind us
we are breathing.

Better than a Gold Watch, the Diamond Heart

*For my friend Balforth Mount, who expanded ways of caring for the
dying, coining the term "palliative care," on his retirement.*

He unpinned the padding from the walls. He took it down
and piled it neatly in a sunlit corner.

He changed the cold metal of the nerve ends to a warm gold,
a softening unto the heart. A warmth where the blizzard blew.
A sheltering from the storm.

He cared in a particularly palliative manner and though trained
to save lives he more saved deaths. So many thousands allowed
to die their own death.

Retiring now, his body of work open at both ends,
his old window has new eyes . . . soft eyes . . .
eyes he has taught to see.
He was what they call in the angel business
a "load lifter."

Linda's hand on his shoulder.

And when his daughter asked for fairies
he gave her fairies.

Not enemies

We are not enemies
though parents told us so

We are not enemies
though they taught us so at school

We are not enemies
just because the pulpit insists

We are not enemies
though strangers toss epithets

We are not enemies
though even love goes sour

We are not enemies
just because we can't contain our pain

We are not enemies
though we meet short of our sameness,
the best of each of us lives in the other.

If we can forgive ourselves
we can forgive anyone.

A little something for the driver . . . for Neal

Some of the old poets whose eyes
have become accustomed to the light,
from whom not even a tear falls or dries on the hot cheek
say that the honey-cat of death enters our breath
in our dreams, slides between images of sunlit
rivers and ladies with stiff fingers drinking tea
and lying about their husbands. . . . They say the world is round
because they have been convinced by mother and the priest
that what is so is so the way they say it is, never other
than birds that only fly, or fish that only swim
but never walked with saints or became saints wriggling
through the mud that connects one phylum with the next . . .

Slides between the parasols and impressionist painters
and the tiny intoxicated dishes full of sorrow
that has not yet quite ripened to misery
and their best works of art . . . Though the family
lies in ruins, "broken cruets," the varnish peeling
from the solid mahogany dinner set . . .
the old Dodge, the sun reached inside
the sheen faded from maroon to tinny red,
the key broken off in the lock, cinderblocks hold
its back feet, the windshield decayed to fog
and rainbows, the driver dead in new shoes
outside of Guadalajara.

Ghalib the sour

That Ghalib is so ecstatically depressed!
He's more depressed than the rusty deity
created by the Romans or the rising
of sandaled feet . . . of course the god
of lightning and all those long identified
in the oaks find sorrow a form of praise
and decided against religion when people
began imagining themselves as separate
from the divine.

Ecstatic devotion turned my litmus heart
bright blue as Krishna, red as the wrists
of the gods of love, some murdered, some
committed to suicide as an act of devotion.

Ghalib says, If every eyelash does not drip
with blood it is not a love story but a fairy tale.

He is agnostic about love like many lovers
and other compulsives who reach
into their pocket and find no bottom,
who have to keep reaching down through
the crust of the earth, down through the hardpan
and crack the roof of the magma chamber
in which their love may be waiting like Eurydice
for Orpheus. And it does not end there
but must keep diving toward the center.

Having pulled themselves up by the nails some societies
believe they are forgiven for atrocities just because
their older brother died that way. Cain blamed Abel.
Ghalib says he can not see how anything he is up to
can end well. His suffering is exquisite.

Some of the gods find his depression attractive,
a show of their power, and rain down on him
peace and joy just to watch him suffer. Lose his
sense of self, his negative attachment to his
lack of ease. His pain he imagines is full
of understanding but it is just the same moldering
salad in the same cracked bowl.

Ah but when love touches this sadness!
without asking anything of it, just offering a
song or a quatrain about the pure nature
of the heart, a bit of Rumi or Kabir perhaps,
shimmering smoke rises, as from an arc welder
when two suitable surfaces come into proximity.
And the longing becomes all there is and
draws us effortlessly into some unexpectedly
comfortable luminosity that needs no name
or title and just acts for the benefit of
the round-shouldered, the bent-necked
and the soul-sad lingerer, the bastion
of the last hope.

Ondrea at 4:00 a.m.

Buddha recommended meditation
in "the third watch of the night"
in that stillness, in that darkness,
the light becomes most intense.

At the dark window numberless faces
dissolve one into the wretched next
in crowds that push forward
for her blessings.
And each gets what they came for,
an open heart attracts the penitent
from other worlds.

Icy rain

The icy rain stings like misdeeds.
Needles stitch the flesh to the frame.
Outside the door is all the difference
in the world, inside no difference.
A candle and a small fire in the iron
box by the single bed. Even somewhat saints
drank wine somewhat to excess but
I have spent that coin and sit by the stream
so my son may be free. I have given
my hat away.

All day long the Tang dynasty is coming
over the telegraph a syllable at a time
reminding me of my dharma ancestors
who hold open for me the door.

Most wrote of the invisible
in what can be seen.
They could be trusted!

Some spoke of only the visible
as real. They walk barefoot
in the morning with a new puppy
in the house to prove their point.
They build their house on charnel grounds.
They burn their cold bodies and turn away.
If they awoke one morning with their
soul in their shoe they would just
shake it out onto the dog's toilet.

Along the paths through the bone-weary mind.
They do not trust anything but their pain.
It makes them feel real.

It was Manifest Destiny that got
my "trike" to the end of the road,
it was the momentum of mind
that decided which way to turn.

The miner hits hardpan—Uh!
The farmer turns what soil remains
after the dry winds—Uh!

The monastic turns the page
and gets it—UH!

The nun removes her habit
and goes out to mother Jesus—UH!

The dervish stops and the world slows on its axis—Uh!

The sailor raises the anchor—Uh!

> This line about the sailor raising the anchor
> is so full of promise as to almost
> invite the deus ex machina
> (the antigravity God machine of the bipolar
> old Greeks' democracy and slaves)
> A machine designed to offer salvation,

even resurrection, as machines are
designed to do. After all Hell
is often preparation for the heavens.

Quixote loved his skinny old horse
but was ambivalent about the wind—Uh!

Hanuman, the son of the wind, wrote
on each of his bones the name of God.
But he needn't have bothered for
God used Hanuman's form to leap faithfully
across the ravine between hemispheres—Uh!

Ichabod Crane found his head
just where Mirabai said it would be
after he cut it off and sat on it, the
whole mind sacrificed for a love
uncontainable—Uh!

When he asked, to what does
"I am" refer, the "I" became a scarecrow
and the amness of awareness filled the questioner
with clarity and delight—the Uh of Being!

Then to what indeed does "Uh!" refer?
The experience of amness, a
warm rain . . .

Basho and Friends

All day long the Tang dynasty is coming
over the telegraph. Their bones lasted
a thousand years, reborn across
the China Sea in Basho,
then took a century or two
to cross the moon-filled Pacific,
arriving straight shouldered
in a new generation of dharma.

Looking directly at those sumi paintings of secluded Taoist mountain retreats it will be noted that Tu Fu, Li Po, Ryokan, Basho and the lot sat perfectly still in a pool of their remnant sorrows and ongoing loneliness until at last the roof fell into the oneness that joined them ever since with all that is.

For the hermit monk-poets, beside the personal loneliness in their four-square mat bamboo hut, there was always waiting by their cold lamp the inheritance of what could be called original loneliness. A boundaryless aloneness, created perhaps when the One is cleaved into the many (or the Big Bang scatters our parts) leaves a strange and reminiscent aftertaste, the homesickness for our original Oneness. It reaches from superficial thought down to the substratum of the psyche. It knows us better than we know ourselves. This essential loneliness knows things about sympathetic joy and loving kindness the heart has yet to reveal to us.

Long before I met Rexroth

Long before I met Rexroth
he pressed two round brass coins into my palm
and told me to sit quietly,
their square mouths spoke Chinese.

In a hundred poems he cracked open
the back of my head and let the Yangtze
float through. He said now it is time
to meet the old man and the young master.
He told me where to wait for Li Po
by the river. And he never failed to show up.
Marvelous! And he pointed to where Tu Fu was
passed out inside a banana tree. Listening carefully
to the cloud layered pagoda of his poem
wet on his lips upon waking.
These guys drank as if they were trying to swallow
the moon floating in their cup of plum wine,
nurturing blossoms at the tip of a bamboo reed.
Being a hermit is lonely business.

Tu Fu knew that cannons behind bamboo barricades
shape the world as surely as tectonic plates
sliding one over another, war cracking the ocean bottom,
draining through, ten thousand silver fish-tails
slapping the cretaceous mud.

Tu Fu asked entrance to Li Po's dreams,
he loved the old man whose perfect cadence
was such an ideal walking speed, whose dreams
chase us still with wild bears and spinning-eyed monks
(or maybe they were ghosts with dharma wheels for eyes)
standing transparently on rock ledges; and panthers
at the harp.

Having spoken of meeting his old friend
beyond the Milky Way when their bones
could no longer speak there is a perfect irony
that like a single note plucked on a lute
which continues forever or a shakuhachi
sticking from a Nike backpack, there is a crater
on the planet Mercury named after Li Po.
You can hear him there sometimes singing.
He says the acoustics are astounding!

Basho watched the dew

Basho was a Japanese poet
of short poems
delicate as a dragonfly wing
solid as paving stones.

He fished with haiku
about worms
instead of worms,
and caught the best of us.

He could cup the sea
in seventeen sensible syllables
a hundred miles away.

He caught the moon in the yellow eye
of an octopus captured in a floating pot.

Basho watched the dew and the cicadas
until they became a word or two
that might convey clarity.

He let nature open the back of his head
and allow a breeze to blow through fresh eyes.

Basho lived on a mountain of one thousand
and one hundred poems; octopi rising
from prehistory with each other in their arms.

His hut was built on the well-worn path taken
by his spiritual ancestors, the hermit poets.
He listened for their quatrains as they passed . . .
they told him to give his longing away
to the willow . . .

Basho was a bit of consciousness hatched
from a thousand year old egg
on whose shell a winter storm can be seen
in Li Po's high passes.

It is a propitious morning for the ink block,
for fish signatures and haiku that stand there in front of you
and looking you straight in the eye rehearse dying.

Basho fished

Basho fished with a pole a string and a hook
He did not care for net-trapped haiku,
he revived syllable by syllable each fish
scale by scale. He was patient.

Poetry trapped in the university,
like spirit trapped in religion,
once freed to the open road,
catches its breath in the long walk-about,
the pilgrimage and the swimming in holy rivers
in a salmon sunrise, alone a lot in the tigered forest
along a solitary path through uncharted territory . . .
soldiers in armor stop by for a moment,
the war-horse paws the ground, ready for more,
but watching the old monk quietly by the silver bend
in the stream the horse settles, the saddle leather
stops creaking under the uneasy warrior whose armor
lies heavy on the quiet body.

A moon-drunk poet by a drunken river,
full moon from bank to bank,
poems littering every writable surface
the rocks are singing of carp,
on the limbs of the cypress round
and round the word "peace"
and on the bare tree trunk
    washed a dozen times
        downstream from the mountains,

the monk's writing table, testing the sumi ink
there is repeated "all is consciousness!" . . .
Following the river bank
stones arranged
in syllables say:

> *The tree*
> *the fish*
> *the monk*
> *all same*
> *all consciousness.*

We are all drunk on the Spring wine
that has little to do with alcohol.
But the waiter whose thumb hangs over the lip
of the cup that leaks glittering constellations
onto the maroon seascape looks vaguely familiar
and smells of the pine and snow of Cold Mountain.

Basho's snow

Basho's snow is at my window
it has been falling for centuries,
it is indifferent to time.

Flakes heavy with the dharma
land perfectly in the present.

Pilgrims nod to each other
silently washing dishes by the window
it is snowing
it will snow forever.

Han Shan has a bonsai
he secretly tends on Cold Mountain,
a hundred year old cypress
begun by his teacher's teacher;
he smiles to himself
when he speaks of non-attachment.

Silence settles on us like a quilt,
the drum abates as the mind quiets—
this silence is of a single piece
and buoys the world despite gravity
and all the metaphors for silence
that silence produces.
  At the bottom of the mouth
just beneath the tongue
Basho slips into the ocean
without a sound.

Meng's mountain

Breathing out I approach the mountain
Breathing in the mountain approaches me.
Following the barely visible
trail through evolution,
following the Milky Way
across the top of the skull
into the star field
at the back of the mind,
pressing forward as sudden
wordless understanding.
My longing is a rope bridge
across icy ravines and empty compliments.
My arms grow tired and fall away,
vertebra by vertebra the hanging gardens drift
up the spine to reveal the 27 heavens.
Bare attention! my face slips from my bare skull,
chest opening to expose Jacob halfway up the ladder.
He longs for the horizon.
So light this passage one must carry
a cicada in each hand to keep the sutras
honest on the lips and in the heart,
that maps the way.

Poems that can hardly wait

There are poems that can hardly wait
Poems that come out of the rocks
Poems we have gone down the center
of flowers to discover
Poems the shape of clouds, poems
that brush the ear and leave for later
in a moment of silent arising
an answer to our longing

Poet Basho, Banana Tree in the Wilderness,
knew stones well, he spoke of the wind
rising from stones, of the cicada song
in the rocks . . . he knew the wild duck, and his spiritual
ancestors looking over his shoulder at the full moon . . .
Basho went for walk-abouts with a backpack
and a staff, stopped in the rain
at a long silver thread swaying
in an autumn wind, clarity was his muse . . .

Basho rattled the Burgermeister's delicate assumptions
and loosened his conceptual reins.
Basho saw each sun, each Buddha at a time
through the fog, Siddhartha in the rain,
Avalokiteshvara in sunsetfire, all wrapped
like the loose wing of summer, dragonfly lace,
around a stalk of last year's deer graze . . .
only as true as the eye.

He saw the timekeeper in the curl of the wave
and heard the cricket whose song has for centuries
taught innumerable shadows bent in bamboo huts.

Basho wrote halfway down the well
that there are Buddhas everywhere
common as daffodils
but there is only one
in the single eye . . .

Ryokan whispers

Li Po's ancestral whisper in Basho
and ourselves speaks out:
Wake up! wake up!
You have been asleep too long,
the bone poets are calling.

It is 6:30 in the morning and the others
have been awake for thousands of years.

The begging bowl is full of Spring
rain and the plop! of Basho's frogs
inherited from Li Po's whisper;
and dreams of town
and the loneliness left over
from the warmth between two candles.

The path to the old hermit hut
is covered with coarse grass
the river, since the ground shook,
has gone to live on the other side
of the mountain. The poems
in falling seeds go unnoticed.

They say the old trail hunters
and the medicine gatherers
have left the mountain of late
and migrated with the rice paddies
to the glossy promise of Beijing
and turned neon blue.
The paths are cleared of nature and go nowhere.
The city lies.

Construction workers gone unpaid jump from
the buildings they have just completed. They
can not go home empty-handed. "Without money
you are a piece of nothing in our country," he said
weeping for his family back in their poor
cozy old village working in other's fields
because he has not been paid and can not
send home fertilizer and seed.

    He said there are no courtyards left.
They have plowed over the Tang and the faint paths
through the bamboo groves have been paved over
just as some "American" schoolyards on tribal lands
were paved over so the earth would be covered,
so the children would not dance and instead
get down to forgetting their native tongue.
The mountain is cluttered with street signs,
The freezing construction workers use the pile of sticks,
the fallen hermit's hut, for kindling while
turning a mountain belonging to tigers and monks
into Sparkling Waters Mountain Resort.

They stop pissing in the stream when
they hear the chanting that comes from under
the fresh laid concrete; but they've been told
to ignore chrysanthemums or starve.

    The terrible loneliness of the hermit leaning
against the empty window now replaced
by the cloying isolation of the homemaker
pacing her empty white concrete square

watching through her picture window
a tableau of well-lit freeways and crowded
boulevards crawling up the mountain
from the sprawling city below.

It is 7:10 and the gray-blue exhaust of
earth-moving machinery chokes down the chant.
It takes a lot of dead dinosaurs to tear the skin off
a mountain, to make a landscape "habitable
for modern man."

In times past it took just a few syllables
from the very edge of Being to send a wave
out into the soul of the world.
But one had to work a whole life,
each day by day, to keep it changed.

The Persians spoke of leaving the marketplace
to enter the Garden, their compass was
a delicate arabesque, an interweaving
of the many into the One, and could tell time
in a variety of realms. The Garden that grew
around the hermit's hut, once empty and returned to time,
has withered and turned to a fine dust;
it has left for the invisible world where,
in the marrow of this world, it is to be found
where bright flowers coincide
on the monk's rough wooden table
in *ikebana*, the art of making
flowers seem to pray.

To town and back

The distance from town to our home
on the side of the mountain
thirty-five miles away
is a thousand miles
and a thousand years.

The pleasantries of a well-made lunch.
New friends, old friends
on the boardwalk through
the shops and trees.
It's a bit like Seurat's picnic, pointedly delightful.
First my life, then yours
we communicate through
the emotional Braille in each other's eyes
like watching the road ahead
wind through the mountains
on the way into
and out of
town.

One does not wish to make a wrong turn
the fall to the valley below
could ruin your day.
The bloodless smile comforts the beast,
suggests harmlessness, curls by the fire.
And the warmth that quickly fills the body,
too quickly, with the safe circle
that closes out the rest of world

and safely translates the inner dialogue.
Laughter and stories. New pets, new poems,
new illnesses. A recipe for each other
prepared right there at the table.
Friendship without gossip another delight.
And the feeling that we almost live
too far from town and the warm glow.

And heading home
past the houses and gardens
past the old trucks in the backyard
and a new one beside the flat house
as the sun drops into a thousand burning windows
and the children are circle dancing,
and the dog retrieving a blue and white striped ball
and the last church
and the last bar and the last house
and the straight streets losing their pavement
becoming winding dirt roads
on the way out of town.

Our minds stretched back to the table,
the friends, the satisfaction.
And should we perhaps live closer
someday
and the trees grow taller
and the valleys deeper
as we climb the mountain . . .

The mind turns down a dirt path
through the aspen grove
and becomes lost beside the Tang streams
and the hermit huts of fine poets.

Li Po is shaking, the poem in him is so strong
it is shaking its way out. It is welcoming us
back to the real world. The murmur
in the forest stills us to listen
yet more quietly to what is being said
by the water to the rocks.

The crows trade quatrains.
A flock of starlings imitates
the wind swirling up from a clearing
to the rumble of Summer in the Spring clouds.

Town is getting farther away.
It seems odd to have ever left the porch
The columbine are opening
An indigo bunting has returned.

And town, well town is quite OK,
a place for inebriation with each other's life
and times
fading now
less distinct with each passing phantasm
around the pebbly bend in the high road.

Heading home with the world
an ocean of breath rising and falling
somewhere along the mountain trails
high in the body.

Leaving our shadow
in a vagrant haiku
on a freshly whitened wall
on the way north out of town.

At 5:00 in the afternoon . . .
for Antonio Machado and sweet Lorca

I

I watch my mind—
It is like a child thinking—
amoebic and sensual,
opening and closing
like an anemone
alone in its briny pool,
thoroughly connected
to the ocean in the tide.

And too long in the shadow, and the sun,
the feral brain stem lays claim to
the world near and far, owning Creation,
its focus tarrying—fascinated—
a floating dust mote,
the sky plated on a puddle,
the light thrown inside;
and below the watery sky
pollywogs wriggle at the peripheries
of the known universe . . .
Awareness a yellow butterfly on a dark flower.
High above a raven's rusty call,
the wind dropping over the lip of the valley,
the crack of a limb off into the woods—

The butterfly alights ever-so-lightly in the wound,
listening, riding the waves of the heart,
wakeful to the child thinking
about thinking; merry-go-round
and round the mulberry bush
ashes ashes all blown away . . .

And Lorca too who fell like a boulder
disturbing the fine dust . . .
and all the dead bulls and their gored *toreadors*
"à la cinco de la tarde". . .

"What have become of your eyes?"
Machado's mother asked,
"I've been asking myself that ever since,"
he recalled . . .

The snap of a limb, a truck accelerates
the mountain road, a distant dog,
a mother coyote on a jackrabbit,
tires sliding toward the edge . . .

The city asks, "What's that sound?"—
It's the wind in the trees in the canyon.

II
Machado asks me for "one or two honest words."

If the poem does not move
when the earth does
it slips a cog and breaks the machine
that wrote it, as close to the soul as love allows.

Is "forgot" an honest word?
Flat as the lid of a coffin,
but already I become unreal
by pretending I know
or pretending I don't.

We do that you know!
become "unreal" I mean—
meaning does that too—
makes us feel almost real,
leads us down the feathery path,
no ground to pretend we're walking on.

"Pretense" is like that too you know . . .
like a hen sitting on an empty nest,
or a boy with a uniform and a gun and tags
indented to fit between dead teeth, in a broken skull.

"War" is like that you know,
gives meaning to broken skulls
and scattered carpals,
pretends in battle colleges
to be a poem (that kills poets).

Lorca, Unamuno, Jimenez, and next Machado eaten
by Moloch and Franco, by the lusty cuspid
and the angry purple vein beneath the turgid tongue.

Although "pretense" is not an honest action
it may be an honest word, protecting nothing.

What is an honest word?

But an honest word is only so
for a moment while still drying on our lips.

The rose is most fragrant just after the shock
of being cut from the stem.

One poet caresses our tombs,
another unwraps a cloud of many colors,
each is trying to get away with his life,
unsuccessfully.

It is not the words that are honest,
it is the lips trembling with love.

Lorca and Whitman dead as Basho, and just as alive

There are a few poems
Basho did not write
that he left for us.

ʃ
With what syllable does Franco stand Lorca
against the wall?
What is the poem found beneath the tongue
in the dead poet's mouth like a love note
left under a pillow? The outline
left in the dust by his last breath.

The thin firing squad of red-boot soldiers
whose fingers fall even now
into their lover's bodies, having finished
their war-stories and their wine . . .
embalmed by sleep joining their comrades
draped over the battlements.

At the killing wall wild animals drop
from bestial dreams and tear the leaves
off the ocean.

Philosophers and academicians who look
at syllables like stirrups, instead of horses,
climb branch to branch through the ocean
carrying papers for their archives
like flamenco roses in their teeth.

And in what words live *Los gentes perdidos*,
lost souls tangled in the leaves and twigs
of time folding back on itself again
as wagons filled with commerce and death
rattle by Whitman's South Street tavern?
He knows the smell of blood and the sound of it in
the iron clad wheels of cannons and wheelchairs;
of young men ruined at Spotsylvania and Bull Run,
at Gettysburg and the Dardanelles, at Waterloo and
the Fields of Flanders, of women and children too
at Wounded Knee and Beirut and phosphorus burning
through their flesh in the midnight canals of Dresden.

We have brutality in our genes and mercy in our heart.
Whitman suffers that smell in his mouth and hands
until he joins the healing dead under the green grass
he likened to grave-markers, relieved
to whisper on the out-breath that "death
is different than anyone imagines, and luckier."

JJ

A gray cat with crème paws takes a culture or two
to cross the room and wakes me from the sleep
I dreamt I was having with my back against
the execution wall. The condemned sing softly
in our native tongues—haiku and cantos,
iambic strategies for peace and Basque love songs,

Arabic and Russian folk ballads,
to offer when we die. Counting our songs
on our fingertips, waiting for a golden wind
to take us oceans away from that blood-soaked wall.

And what remains after the singers are silenced?
The last prayers and the blue vein under the tongue
the spirit used to translate the first light into dawn.
And the howl of the celestials the closer to the wall one stands.

I am breathed by Lorca's voice lost in a drop
of water and the miscreancy of his crickets.
He broke the dance into stanzas that could not stay apart,
they loved each other so, and joined back together,
too remarkable to be understood without reference
to the light, where its flowering vine penetrates
my chest and sets roots in my heart.
There the poem grows
into whatever is hidden inside it.

Friends looking for Lorca's grave, said it disappeared
over the edge into a ravine. They said the local pub
had a dry mouth when asked where the angel was buried.
So they put their ear to the ground and heard
the songs of earthworms tending the shrine of his corpse,
taking Eucharist from his delicious thumb . . .

Translators and alchemists are often similarly motivated.
Neither are able to tell the whole truth, like Einstein
on the intuitive scrap it took a century to translate
and is still more felt than known on the other side,
the warm side of the dark stained wall
where life comes out from under and is carried
by the wind across the crevasse between hemispheres,
the corpus callosum, across which Himalayan climbers
place Jacob's ladder. The devoted climber crosses
on hands and knees.
The disheartening dreams
    we hid in our ambitions
    no longer support our weight;
    only knowing as the seeker may
    the effect of love on matter.

III
When the top of the head opens
dread is an accomplishment

Something hidden is revealed
beyond the edge of the doubt
that blocks delight

Climbing, the wall grows taller,
all the ended lives walk the parapets.

All along the watchtower ghosts
and the river lost in tangled banter
and the loves who took the knife
and the monk who took needles
until he burst and his wife caught fire.

The gods have to draw straws again
to see who is tyrant and who is healer,
who is poet and who is executioner, who carries
messages, and who takes liberties;
who never dies and who barely makes it into form
repeatedly falling away.

We can not force the depths,
we can not storm the gates of Paradise,
it will break our spirit.

The sun follows the superstition of blue
across the arc of summer
and the world comes to an end
just the way it began yesterday.